Who isn't charmed by an inspiring fairytale?

Who isn't captivated by a wonderful love story?

Who doesn't love a happy ending?

This particular love story is like nothing you've ever read before. Two unlikely lovers — a three-legged cat named Henry and a two-legged dog named Tink — meet most unexpectedly, in classic Hollywood "cute meet" style.

Tink is unlike any girl Henry's ever met — and at first he doesn't know quite what to make of her. "Who *is* this amazing creature, with her effervescent energy?" he wonders.

And Tink is curious about this strong, silent guy — with his great hair. "Who *are* you?" she wonders as she moves closer to get a better look at this fine feline fellow.

The story is first and foremost about self-discovery, acceptance, and how what may seem impossible to some becomes a reality. It is the meeting of two innocent souls who don't see each other as "different," but realize that we are all "different" in our own way and we are all special in our own way. In working through this discovery, feelings of admiration, love, and compassion are born and these two "souls" bond as best friends.

The story of their meeting is one of love-almost-at-first-sight, as they are intrigued and entranced — rather than put off — by the differences they see in each other. As they get acquainted, with a nuzzle here and a purr there, their hearts touch…and both are transformed. And the rest, as they say, is history.

This true love story of Henry and Tink will captivate kids of all ages, from 3 to 93. Read it and reap…a belly full of laughter and a heart full of love.

HENRY AND TINK
A REMARKABLE ROMANCE

To those who choose love and compassion

Cathy Conheim and BJ Gallagher

Written by Cathy Conheim and BJ Gallagher
Photography by Cathy Conheim and Belinda Hein
Design and Editorial by Mercedes Sironi
Graphics by Ginny Schumacher of *Designs by Ginny*

Henry and Tink
A Remarkable Romance

Breakthrough Press
P. O. Box 135
La Jolla, CA 92038

Visit us at Henrysworld.org

Once upon a time,
　　in the not-so-distant past,
　　　　a puppy was born
　　　　　　– an unusual little dog.

It was clear from the very start
　　that she was no ordinary pup
　　　　– everyone could see this was so.

For ordinary pups have four legs,
　　and this one
　　　　had only two.

"How can a dog walk
with only two legs?"
the breeder said.

"No, no, this is no good.
The dog will have to go."

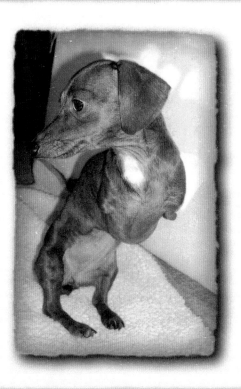

He didn't understand
that when you're different,
it doesn't mean
you're no good.

Fortunately, a nice family
heard about the special pup
and came to see her.

"Oooh, she's darling,"
they said.

"Yes, we will adopt her
and love her as our own."

And so it came to pass –
the pup went to live
with her new family.

"What shall we name her?"
    they asked one another.

After some discussion
    they decided on "Tink"–
        a very small name
            for a very small dog.

The name was perky and playful,
    just like the pup.

Tink had a big spirit,
    in a tiny body.

With just two legs,
  she still went
    wherever she wanted.

She would stand up
  on her two back legs,
    then dive forward,
      landing on her tiny chest.

Again and again,
  cheerful as could be,
    Tink would stand up,
      dive forward,
        and thunk! . . .
          land right
            on her chest.

She bounced to and fro
    she bounced up and down
        so much you could almost
            hear her thoughts.

    "I tink I can,
    I tink I can,
    I tink I can."

This
    pup
      was
        clearly
          going
            places
              in
                life.

One day, Tink's family surprised her.

"We've met some new friends," they said, "and we're going to visit them."

"You get to come, too!"

Tink just loved adventures
and she wiggled happily
as they put her
in her pretty
snuggly carrier.

When they arrived at
their new friends' house,
they took Tink out of her
carrier and let her
explore.

It was a wonderful house,
full of new sights and sounds,
and best of all, smells . . .

Tink sniffed here, there,
and everywhere,
bouncing on her chest
from place to place.

Suddenly she saw something
that stopped her in her tracks.

What's this?
she thought
as she looked intently.

Is it a dog?
she wondered.

If it's a dog,
he's even more different
than I am.

He's got three legs
instead of four,
or two,
like me.

I've got to take a closer look . . .

With that,
  Tink bounced
    toward the odd stranger.

But the stranger scampered
  further away –
    startled by Tink's bouncing.

Who is that?
he wondered as he jumped
onto a chair.

*Nobody told me
we were having company.*

*And why
is she bouncing
like that?*

Now it was Tink's turn
  to be startled.

> *How is he jumping*
> *around like that?*
>   she wondered.

> *He's got only three legs*
> *but he can really fly.*

She bounced closer,
  determined to meet
    this unusual stranger.

> *I tink I can,*
> *I tink I can,*
> *I tink I can,*

> she sang to herself
>   as she bounced forward.

By now, the three-legged stranger
was curious too.

She's kind of charming,
    he thought to himself,
in an odd kind of way.

He jumped down from the chair
    to meet the puppy
        bouncing toward him.

"Who are you?"
    he asked,
        as they came nose to nose.

"And where do you come from?"

"*My name is Tink,*"
she answered.

"*And who are YOU?*"
she asked.

"*My name is Henry, JM
and I'm a cat,*"
he replied.

"*I live here.*"

"*A cat!*" Tink exclaimed.

"*I've never met a cat before.*"

"*Do all cats have three legs?*"
she inquired.

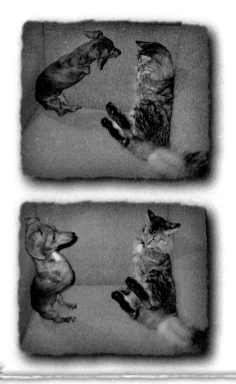

"*No,*" Henry replied.
"*They almost always have four.*"

"*But I'm **special**,*" he declared.
"*That's why I have the
JM after my name . . .*

*I'm Henry **Just Me**.*"

"*Do you think I'm special too?*"
Tink asked in a tiny voice.

"*Well, you're different . . .
like me,*" he said softly.

"*But then . . .
everyone is different,*"
Henry thought outloud.

There was a long pause.
Henry looked at Tink.
Tink looked at Henry.

*"So . . . that means EVERYONE
is special in his or her own way,"*
they whispered to each other.

Henry and Tink knew
    from that moment on
        that they would be
           best friends
              forever.

She nuzzled him
    with her muzzle,
        as dog's do
           when they show affection.

He licked her
    with his sandpaper tongue,
        as cats do
           when they show affection.

Henry and Tink
 were quite the pair

  – cuddling,
   sniffing,
    and licking –

sweetly getting to know each other.

"I'm a little tired," Tink said.

*"All that bouncing
you do to get around
looks like a lot of work,"*
said Henry.

*"Why don't you rest here?
You can have my bed
for a cat nap,"* Henry said.

As Tink snuggled in for a cat nap
—er, *dog* nap –
she closed her eyes,
stretched out her
two tired legs,
and relaxed her little body.

She drifted off into gentle slumber.
And as often happens
when doggies sleep,
she began to dream.

She dreamed that she and Henry
were playing and having fun.

She dreamed of Henry
flying from place to place
with his strong
hind legs.

And she dreamed that suddenly
　　she was moving very fast,
　　　　all around,
　　　　　　everywhere.

As fast as
　　she wanted to go,
　　　　she could go.

As Tink dreamed,
　　her two little legs twitched –
　　　　this, too, often happens
　　　　　　when doggies dream.

Tink began to hear voices
in her dream –
someone calling her name:

"Tink, wake up, little one."

She quickly recognized
the voice of her Mom.

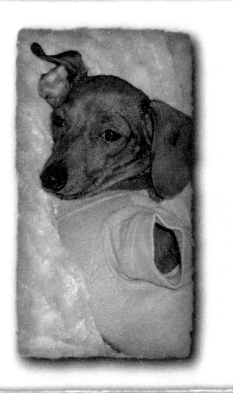

She opened her eyes to see that
Henry was still by her side,
watching over her.

And her Mom
was sitting on the floor,
holding a gadget with wheels.

Tink blinked a few times
    and yawned as she roused
        from her nap.

"Tink, we have a surprise for you,"
        Mom said.

"We have wheels for you," she said.

"See?"

"This is a set of wheels made just for YOU," her Mom continued.

"Now you won't have to bounce on your chest anymore!"

Tink couldn't believe her sleepy little eyes.
Mom strapped the set
of wheels around Tink,
as Henry watched
with curious eyes.

"There!"
her Mom said.

"Give the wheels a try!"

It took all of 30 seconds
for Tink to figure out
how to move with the wheels.

The next thing you know,
she took off like a rocket
across the lawn!

"Woo Hoo!"
she yipped.

"Look, Mom, no paws!"
she called out in excitement.

Henry watched in wonder.
He jumped up
on the counter top
to get a better view
(and avoid being run over!)

He had never seen
   such a beautiful sight –
      this gentle pup
         zooming around,
            faster than any dog
               –or cat–
            he'd ever seen.

The joy he felt warmed him
   from the top of his ears
      to the tip of his tail.

He looked at tiny Tink
   and his heart
      swelled with happiness
         and pride.

Tink felt the emotion too . . .
　　　She loved her new wheels.
　　　　　She loved her wonderful family.
　　　　　　　And she loved Henry most of all –

　　　this unusual cat,
　　　　　so gentle
　　　　　　　and kind.

Tink's dream had come true . . .
　　　her dream of running free,
　　　　　and being loved
　　　　　　　the way she is.

25

She now understood
that love has no limits
— even without limbs.

And Tink found happiness . . .
only as Tink could.

THE END . . . ?

NO, JUST THE BEGINNING.

Tink's Kibble for Thought

- Everyone is special in his or her own way.

- Love comes when you least expect it.

- Believe "I think I can."

- Love knows no boundaries.

- Practice love, kindness, and compassion.

- Open your hearts and minds to new things.

Henry's Kibble for Thought

- Hard things happen.

- Play the hand you are dealt.

- Be "Just You."

- Hate is learned.

- Love follows no rules.

- Believe in love, kindness, and compassion.

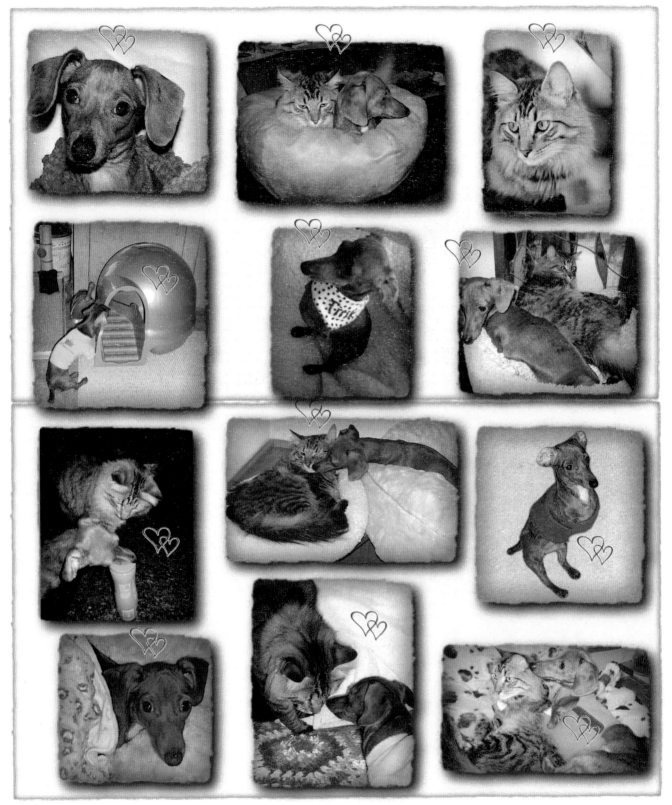

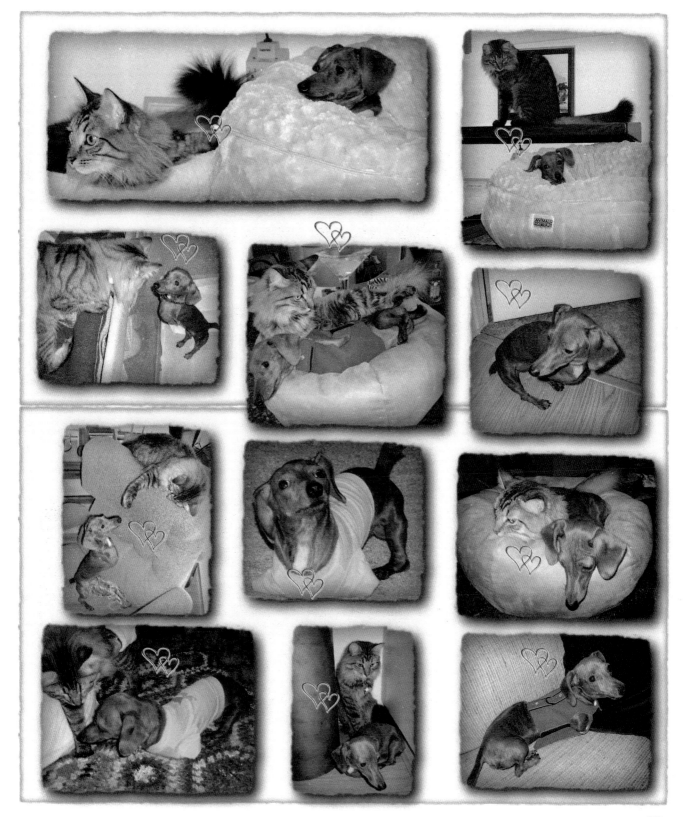

To Tink...

Roses are Red
Violets Are Blue
My new Love's a dog
Her legs are but two

Together we play
We more than have fun
She bounces to find me
Boy, can she run!

Some say we're disabled
But not Tink and I
We play like all others
The time it does fly

She stands on two legs
And I stand on just three
Two Kindred spirits
Tink and Just Me!

For those that "tink" Tink
Is not more than just swift
Let me remind you
To me she's a gift

What limbs one's endowed with
Is not really the point
It's what's in our hearts
That our souls do anoint

So Tink is my playmate
And also my love
A two-legged doggie
Sent down from above

Forget what is missing
Be here and now
Count all your blessings
We'll show you how

So all you dear humans
Who come watch us play
Remember what matters
Live fully each day!

Love,

Henry jm

Hand-crocheted
Henry and Tink dolls
available at
www.henrysworld.org

Purchase our Love Series cards and Love Poem bookmark at
www.henrysworld.org

Henry and Tink

FREE Online Resources

- Henry and Tink Puppets--paper-bag models

- Activity Sheet--mazes and word searches

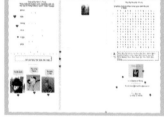

- Placemat--word scramble, dot-to-dot, etc.

Just Me . . .

- Henry's Song

You can download these FREE resources at www.henrysworld.org

Henry and Tink

FREE Online Resources

- Finger Puppets--each one displaying an emotion

I'm shy

I'm happy

I'm scared

I'm angry

- "Ouch!" Emotional Bandage
  App available on iTunes

I'm confused

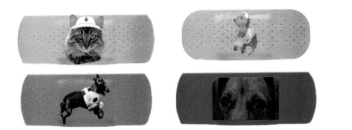

You can download these FREE resources at www.henrysworld.org

CATHY CONHEIM and BJ GALLAGHER are story tellers. They believe that storytelling is the way we connect with others and with what is essential in our lives. People forget facts and figures but they remember good stories.

CATHY has always felt that a loving heart can overcome incredible obstacles, and she loves to help people achieve their goals and dreams. She has been a therapist, speaker, author, coach and consultant and, most recently, cat scribe for Henry. She is proud of being a catalyst for change, and is founder and producer of the Real Women Project, which reached the eyes and ears of 40 million people worldwide. Cathy lives in her mountain-top home in La Jolla with Donna, Dolly and, of course, Henry. You can reach her at www.henrysworld.org.

BJ likes to tell people that she "writes kids' books for grownups," including her best-seller, *A Peacock in the Land of Penguins* (now in 19 languages), and her newest book, *The Power of Positive Doing*. She writes business parables, women's books, stories for kids, poetry, gift books, and a line of greeting cards. BJ lives in her magic tree house in Los Angeles with her dog Fannie, her three cats, and two rabbits. You can reach her at www.bjgallagher.com.

Photographs: Cathy Conheim www.henrysworld.org